Smiles for Seniors

(And Anyone Else Who Can Poke Fun at Themselves)

by Edie Landau

Illustrated by Tina Landau

1

For my Mother

From her Daughter

With all the love in the world

ACCEPTANCE

At first, it felt awkward and hard to say,

It never came out in a natural way.

Now, it rolls off my tongue with the greatest of ease,

As I proudly request, "Senior Discount, please."

TIVO

My Universal Remote can perform almost any task.

Record?   Delete?   Fast Forward?   Just ask.

But there's one function I fervently wish it could do.

Can it be programmed to Re-wind a year or two?

ON MEETING AN OLD FRIEND

We stood and hugged, and then we kissed,

We told each other how much we were missed.

She told me, "You haven't aged a single bit.

You look younger than ever.   Come, let's sit."

I told her, "And you are ageless - still so vital and spry."

How easily we both have learned to lie!

WITH APOLOGIES TO STEPHEN SONDHEIM

I feel pretty, oh, so pretty,

I feel pretty and witty and gay,

Cause I just got my hair tinted,

and no one can see the gray.

OH, LORD, HEAR MY PRAYER

"From your lips to God's ears."

my mother used to say,

Today that expression

has become passé.

Cause He's either not listening

as much as He should,

Or maybe it's simply

that His hearing ain't good.

Sometimes our abilities

with age do fade.

So I'm thinking maybe God

needs a hearing aid!

LISTEN MY CHILDREN
AND YOU SHALL HEAR....

I know I've already told you this story,

You've heard quite a few from my repertory,

But it's such fun to remember "way back when"

Would you indulge me while I tell it again?

EASY!!!!!!!!

"How do you stay looking so young?"

they earnestly implore,

I answer, "It just takes longer –

and costs a helluva lot more."

SCHOOL DAZE

When it comes to landmark dates I wish still exist,

The "first day of school" is at the top of my list.

A VISIT TO THE EYE DOCTOR

We finished the right eye,
and the conversation was like a game,

We switched to the left eye,
and he once more did proclaim,

"Just tell me which is better. (CLICK) This one...
(CLICK)...or this?

"I still think they're the same,"
I responded with a hiss.

       (Mmmmm, this is getting pretty bad...)
       (What's more, I think he's getting mad.)

"But which is better? No. 1...(CLICK)...
or No. 2 (CLICK)?" he'll repeat,

And, finally, I stop hedging
and go down in sad defeat.

And then I'm consumed by worry
throughout the examination long...

What will the outcome finally be,
if my answers were all wrong?

DRIVING NIGHTMARES

The fear of road rage keeps me from honking my horn,

And the choice words I wanna scream remain unsworn.

But my middle finger I stick up in the air... yes, so be it.

I just make sure my hand's in my lap so he can't see it.

And then I flee it!

HAIR TODAY, GONE TOMORROW

I read that gelatin is good for women's hair loss,

So a heaping teaspoon into my juice I do toss.

While I admit it has helped where my hair grows thin,

It also sprouts hairs on my chinney, chin chin!

"A" IS FOR APPLE

When I said I was going to the Apple store,

 it was not for my laptop's sake.

I went to buy Macintosh's...

for the Thanksgiving pie I'm going to bake.

BEFORE SCHOOL STARTS

It's that time of year –

their suitcases are slammed shut.

They tell me the kids need a vacation –

but vacation from what?

THE BIG BAD WOLF

I'll huff and I'll puff,

while I push off my seat,

And if I get lucky,

I

will

land

on

my

FEET.

SCHOOL FOR SENIORS

The class was called "Safety Tips for Older Folks."

Well, I'm here to tell you it was a hoax.

"Be aware of your surroundings" is the
  number 1 rule -

For Younger Folks that guide might be cool.

But we elders in the dark, see nothing but black,

Cause 20-20 vision, believe me, we lack.

And noises don't register, cause we don't hear
so well,

We also suffer from a poor sense of smell.

We're told to buy a whistle and in our tote bags
stow it.

Except we Seniors don't have the breath to blow it.

If all else fails, we're told to run. Run? Me run?

Well, after that "brilliant" advice, I knew I
was done!!!

So I seriously thought about it and made a decision.

I'm just going to stay home at night
and watch television.

HAVE YOU HEARD THE ONE ABOUT...

We've all had them.

As a "senior moment" they are known,

They thrust you into

an unearthly zone,

But the episode that proves

to be most repelling,

Is... forgetting the punch line

to the joke you are telling.

GRAMMAR GIRL

I recognize when the word "its" an apostrophe lacks;

When "there/their" get confused by newspaper hacks.

Whether it should be "hear" or "here" I'm always sure.

And the use of "your" for "you're" I can't endure.

But my communication skills are growing weak,

Because I never did learn how to speak "geek."

I'm considered old hat. I must take a back seat,

Because I also don't blog and I don't even tweet.

A SHORT SHORT TALE

As we get older, our spines compress,

And I've lost a few inches, I must confess.

So when next I go out for a sushi treat,

I'll just ask the hostess for a booster seat.

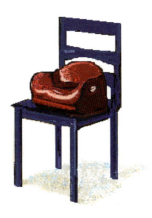

SMARTPHONES FOR SMART PEOPLE

A "smartphone."   Oh, what an invention!

Well, I have degrees too numerous to mention.

So I made the purchase, but I simply can't use it,

My clumsy fingers just seem to abuse it.

Am I unique? Do I stand alone,

waiting for Apple to make a "dumbphone"?

WHADDAYA SAY?

Of course I hear you! Loud and clear!

As long as you speak into my good ear!

CHECK-IN TIME

I used to crave certain luxuries

in my hotel room...

A fresh rose in a vase,

about to bloom...

A make-up mirror

that swings out and in...

Ear pads

to obliterate any hallway din...

A telephone in the bathroom,

strategically placed...

A top sheet

whose border is delicately laced.

Also, I'm always pleased

by a boxed shower cap,

And maid service

that tidies up after my nap.

And, of course, the chocolates

on the pillow every night,

And bedside lamps,

both on the left and the right.

But now the luxury that makes me happiest by far

Is the shower that's outfitted with a strong grab bar!!!

SPRING CLEANING

I made up my mind... if I haven't worn it in a year,

it's going to Goodwill!

The anticipation of "closet-cleansing"

gives me a thrill,

I take out the leather jacket

with shoulder pads, so high and so wide,

And then the flowered mini skirt

I once wore with pride.

> (That's when I was oh, so young and
>
> starry-eyed.
>
> And more important, when I was also very
>
> firm-thighed.)

I take out the colorful muumuu

I picked up in the Pacific,

And that fringed Woodstock blouse

I once thought was terrific.

I take out the maxi raincoat

that has long gone out of style.

And the school-girl sweater set...

and add them ALL to the pile.

I keep on sorting... the collection does expand

and mount,

The cast-offs lie on my bed...

far too many to count!

When I started this task,
 I was relatively happy,
But now looking at my "hand-me-downs"
makes me feel crappy.
And my donor's remorse
slowly festers... and grows,
As I think of my history reflected
in all of those clothes.
I console myself: "I'll never wear them again,
so help me God!"
Then I lovingly hang them
back on my clothes closet rod.

OH, NO!!!!!!

Of all the rude awakenings,

the one that cannot be beat,

Is when an elderly woman

offers you her subway seat.

THE SECOND AMENDMENT TO THE UNITED STATES CONSTITUTION

The right to "bare" arms

is an inalienable right,

But my arms are flabby,

so I keep them out of sight!

LOVE RESURRECTED

I have to admit that I've been in this
relationship before,

But I've travelled far from that turbulent shore,

And when our union ended, I said "Amen."

And I'm not sure I'm ready to jump in again.

But when his eyes looked up and connected
with mine,

I trembled and thought, "I'm gonna cross
the line!"

When my fingers rumpled his silky head,

And when I saw him curled up on his cozy bed,

My resolve collapsed like a water-drenched
noodle,

And I went home with a 12-week old poodle.

HAPPY BIRTHDAY

Another birthday!!
Champagne down
the hatch!
From here on in,
It's patch, patch, patch.

IT'S HUMAN ORIGAMI

I'm going
to stand up –
please put your
horses on hold,
It may take a few minutes
for me to unfold.

THE EDUCATION OF...

I took a Speed Writing Course –

now my pencil doth fly,

I took a Speed Reading Course –

and the pages whiz by.

But there's another talent

I would like to master.

I want a Speed Course

to teach me "How To Hear Faster."

GET READY, GET SET...

I constantly try to be

the first one out of the gate,

Cause if I'm always early,

I can never be late.

READY!
(JUST GIMME A MINUTE...
OR TWO...OR THREE)

I used to time it – five minutes to get ready
after I got out of bed,

Pull up the jeans, step into clogs,
T-shirt over the head.

Done! I won!

But at this point in time,
when I'm not getting any stronger,

Facing the day takes me longer...and longer...
and longer,

Hooking my bra with a torn rotater
in my right shoulder,

Confirms that I'm getting older...and older...
and older.

My elasticized knee-highs take forever
to pull over my heel.

(Who dreamed swollen ankles could be
such a big deal?)

And then there's the problem of bending down
to buckle my shoes.

(My back cries out for a shot of booze!)

And trying to manipulate a metal clasp
with an arthritic thumb,

Is a challenge I've not been able to quite overcome.

So, Dear Lord,

If an emergency is coming that requires a quick exit,

I'd feel very blessed,

If you didn't let it happen until after I'm dressed.

●　　　●　　　●

THE LURE

Wanna know why my grandkids
are so eager to visit me?

I'll give you the answer ...
I'll give you the key.

"PIZZA IS NOT DINNER!"
is their mother's parenting style.

While I've programmed Domino's
on my handy speed dial.

RESORTS

Their ads tout hiking, tennis, golf and all that pap,

But they never ever mention great places to nap.

MY FRED ASTAIRE

He's eager to get up on the floor,

each and every time,

He's loved to dance –

since way back in his prime,

So whether the band is playing

a samba, a rumba, or something else hot,

We are always dancing

his usual foxtrot.

TWO HAS-BEENS

We both have aged - but not too well.

Of our former selves, we're just a shell.

We used to be firm, we used to be sleek,

Now, sad to say, we both do creak.

Our deep rich colors have mostly faded,

We both now need to get upgraded.

We are sagging.   Of our former chic, we are shorn,

We've been through the mill, & we're both shop-worn,

Where we once were taut, we now are bumpy.

Where we once were smooth, we now are lumpy.

Who's the more tattered, I will not vouch.

Is it me or is it my couch?

MATURE DRIVERS

I used to hate drivers,

who drove too slow.

And in my frustration,

my horn I would blow.

And when a driver hesitated

to make a turn on red,

I'd shout out my window,

"GO! It's legal, Dumb-head!"

And when they lingered

at a stop sign for a minute or two,

I'd often go around them

and drive right through.

But age

    has converted me

       and I've crossed

         the line,

That slow Honda

    they're now

      honking at,

        I admit, is mine.

SHOP 'TIL YOU DROP

The boots won't go on,

Though the shoe salesman tries,

I gotta buy jeans –

I need the next size.

I can't get my bra hooked

across my back.

The dress I just bought

looks more like a sac,

I got into a bathing suit –

but with so many wiggles!

I'm giving up the beach –

too much of me jiggles,

My favorite skirt must be let out –

yes, quite a bit,

      But I'm pleased that my earrings

from high school still fit!

OPENING XMAS PRESENTS

I open the next box

on my Xmas gift pile.

Oh, God, I hate it...

It's an old lady's style.

I detest that look,

and the color's all wrong,

(Why does no one ever buy me

a sexy thong?)

But I'll say "I love it"

and swallow a happy pill -

And tomorrow I'll donate it...

To the nearest goodwill.

DINING AL AERO

Reports of a more pleasant flight
are totally fallacious.
Since airlines stopped serving meals,
the aromas are outrageous.
The passenger on my right just dropped
a meatball in his lap,
The guy on my left is devouring
a chicken curry wrap.
Across the aisle, a girl's munching
a garlic pizza slice.
Her neighbor's take-out container wafts
Orange Chicken/Rice.
Surviving these olfactory assaults
is a major task.
Next time I board, I'm bringing...
a World War I gas mask.

WHO, SIR? I, SIR?
YES, SIR. YOU, SIR.

I'm always the Designated Driver

chosen by "My Crowd."

Bearing this special moniker

makes me very proud.

It's not because I'm sober

(though that would be all right)

It's cuz I'm the only person

who can still drive at night.

WHAT A DEAL!

Early Sunday mornings, the newspaper's
delivered to my door.

National News, Book Reviews, The Arts...
and so much more.

I read the articles until the clock tolls eleven,

Then, scissors in hand, bask in Coupon Heaven!

During the week, I indulge all my cravings,

And I smile as the register
tolls up my savings.

MY FAIR LADY

I could have danced all night.

Yes, I <u>could</u> have danced all night,

Except that my satin pumps are now too tight.

And my knees both creek and my back is sore.

Guess Ginger Rogers I ain't gonna be no more.

IN AND OUT

To achieve success, the guru implores,

Upon entering and exiting life's many doors,

You'll avoid being branded a bumbling fool,

If you learn when to push and when you should pull.

EATING OUT

Yes, it's an "in" restaurant – there's always a line.

Yes, the service is impeccable, the food is divine.

But there is a dress code, I want to make it clear,

You need to be wearing...plugs in your ear.

THE BEST AND THE WORST

The world's happiest sound that wafts to the rafter,

Is the universal delight of a little child's laughter.

And the world's nastiest sound, piercing and shrill,

Is the persistent drone of a dentist's drill.

MY JURY DUTY

The two attorneys prattled on - they could not agree,

But all I could think about was "I gotta pee!"

A CUP OF JOE

Starbucks is one of the things I vowed not to do,

I was perfectly happy with the coffee I brew,

Then I succumbed to their ad:

"Iced Mocha Caramel, rich and creamy"

And I must confess, it was pretty dreamy.

(Oh, how I wish I hadn't picked it,

Because sadly now I am addicted!)

GETTING TO KNOW YOU

In some societies, people define you
by your college degree,

Or by the cheeses you serve – Velveeta or Brie?

Or perhaps you're defined by your wedded wife,

Or perhaps by how you hold your fork and knife.

Or by your address - ah, that's at the top of the list,

Or by the shoes that you wear - get the gist?

But I live in Los Angeles, where <u>how</u> you may thrive,

Is definitely defined by the car that you drive.

MR. KNOW-IT-ALL

I've learned from geniuses
and I've been inspired by hacks,
Yet my basic education
certain knowledge still lacks,
It's that deepest mystery of life,
which I aim to decode:
Just why did the chicken cross the road?

EASY TO OPEN

The instructions read, "Pull the Tab."

But where's the piece you're supposed to grab?

And why isn't a milk carton easy to open -

Without all that pushin', pressin' and gropin'?

And how about the vial with a child-proof cap?

Which arthritic fingers can't seem to snap?

And how about the items embedded in plastic,

That require strength Herculean and drastic?

Americans are smart - we sent men to the moon,

So why are packagers

so out of tune?

THE CARD GAME

I'm hosting a bridge game – it goes very well,

But a half hour in, comes the killer bombshell.

Cause there's always one player who gets a bit huffy.

"Can we open a window, the air here's so stuffy."

I slide open the window, and we go on with the bid,

But there's always one player, who will not be outdid.

"There's a draft coming in to the place where I sit,

Can we close that window just a wee bit?"

I slide the window a little, and we go on with the play,

Then suddenly a new voice enters the fray,

"I'm hot! Doesn't your air conditioning work?"

"Her conditioner's too noisy," one player does smirk.

"Okay, then may I suggest a different plan?"

She looks at me: "Do you have an old-fashioned fan?"

That does it!   No more foursomes for me!

Not even a <u>PAIR</u>!

From this moment on,

I play only solitaire!

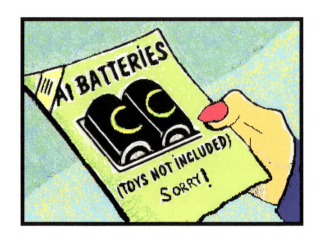

LOOK AT THE LABEL

The Battery instructions read, "Requires Two C's."

But all I had were those big fat D's.

I stocked up on C's in one quick breeze,

But everything new requires 9-V's.

So many times I have been deluded!

I now buy only "BATTERIES INCLUDED."

MUSIC TO MY EARS

The most beautiful sentence, if I could pick it,

Would be, "Yes, we validate your parking ticket."

LOG IN

I better put them in my head,

fix them with glue,

So that I can say them correctly

to the Celestial Crew.

Because the Pearly Gates sentry

won't open the latch,

If my user ID and my password

don't match.

S.O.S.

Because I am trapped in Cyber space Hell!

And tell me, please, what is a "URL" ?????????

My printer warned me it's low on ink,

My answer machine is on the blink.

Though the booklet I did diligently cram,

My Fax keeps flashing, "PAPER JAM!"

My cell phone shows 2 messages which aren't there,

My "user names" are stored, but I can't find where.

(Or maybe it's my "password" I should have used,

I really don't know – I'm too confoozed.)

I give up!!!!!!!!

I'm going back to the tape player I can use
with ease.

I'm buying a typewriter that for me was a breeze.

I've put ink in my trusty Waterman pen,

Which I haven't used since God knows when.

I've retrieved my note cards, ivory and pure,

You'll be getting "snail mail" from me you can
be sure.

Yes, I'm a dinosaur, I'm proud to say,

And in Antediluvia I'm gonna stay!

My frustration is huge, my patience is short,

Please help me.   I need immediate support.

No, not financial.   I'm getting by Okay.

No, not physical.   All my limbs are in play.

But I need support, because I am a wreck.

The support that I need is digital tech.

GOOD NIGHT, SLEEP TIGHT

After a hectic day, when my nerves are jangled,

And my brain feels tight – like it's been mangled,

And a gigantic "To Do" list in my head still hovers,

I sip some tea and then slip under my covers.

I've studied relaxation exercises so I first go that route:

 I breathe in deeply, and I slowly breathe out.

Then to chant my "oms" I don't hesitate,

As I free up my body to meditate.

But if after an hour, sleep is still distant and far,

I do my stretches, while reaching…

for my valium jar.

WHO KNOWS?

Of friendly advice, there is never a dearth,

But how do I decide whose viewpoint has worth?

Especially when it comes to a serious matter,

And all that I'm hearing is idle chatter.

The counsel I'm receiving is widely varied,

No wonder I'm feeling helpless and harried.

I once knew the right answer, but, alas, I forgot...

For my aching back, do I apply cold? Or apply hot?

DOCTOR, LAWYER,
MERCHANT, CHIEF

If I could re-invent myself,

my occupation I would switch,

I'd choose to be a philanthropist

(Cause it would mean that I was rich!)

VOCABULARY VULGARITIES

I used to be straight-laced and somewhat of a prude,

Certain words were unacceptable – I considered them rude,

I had very strict rules about what language was proper,

If one of my daughters said even "damn," I forcibly stopped her.

But I have moved a million miles away from that somber position,

And I am happily ensconced in "profanity remission."

God, it feels so liberating to spew the word "Shit,"

And I'm not embarrassed by saying it – not one little bit.

Spouting "Just suck it up!" now gives me great pleasure,

Even the F-word has become a verbal treasure.

That grouchy woman down the hall, I used to call a "witch,"

Well, I have re-christened her – I now call her "Bitch!"

And when I'm angry, are there any words I may have missed,

That more aptly describe my feelings than, "I am pissed"?

So I hope you're not offended, because you think it's taboo,

If you are, I'll say, "Sorry." But I'll be thinking "Oh, screw you!"

MEMORIES

We were boyfriend/girlfriend in our teens,

We believed our attraction was in our genes.

He gave me a necklace, which held half a heart,

So I'd never forget him when we were apart.

It wasn't silver, and it certainly wasn't gold,

It was just cheap plastic, if truth be told.

But I still keep that relic in my jewelry chest,

And sometimes I look at it, when I feel distressed.

We went separate ways to seek fortune & fame.

And today I can't even remember his name!

LOVE LETTERS

I'm warmed by hugs and kisses =

they never fail.

Except when they come

(xoxo)

via email

MY PERSONAL PHARMACY

Is this one twice a day - or just one at night?

They all lie before me - a formidable sight,

They look like a rainbow – each and every hue.

One-a-Day is red, but my Estrogen's blue,

The white calcium tablet I'm supposed to chew.

And my orange aspirin I can masticate too.

But is this the one I must take with a meal?

Or on an empty stomach? Oh, what is the deal?!?

The print is too small for me to read.

So what directions am I supposed to heed?

Capsule? Or caplet? Perhaps a soft gel?

Forgeddabout it! I'm suddenly feeling quite well.

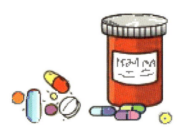

COLOR ME MINE

It would take a lot of goodies to tickle me PINK.

But GREEN to the "gills?" - what is that link?

I could be GREEN with envy, or I could have a GREEN thumb

I could be lacking in GREY matter, which might make me dumb.

I might have – could have – to the PURPLE been born,

But a BLUE-blood moniker, I never have worn.

I've never rattled on till I was BLUE in the face.

I'm not running a BLUE streak in a marathon race.

I'm not a RED hot Mama, nor involved in RED tape.

I'm certainly not a RED neck in any manner or shape.

I don't do BROWN nosing, it's not my style.

I'm not a YELLOW Belly, brimming with guile.

Ah yes, Technicolor is brilliant and bright.

But I was produced in black and white.

DOWN FOR THE COUNT

When did I become a "used-to-be"?????

It happened in a second – one, two, three!

No one now asks me, "What do you do?"

In their heads, they've decided that I am through.

I once was defined by many esteemed names,

But my personal stature has gone down in flames.

I'm no longer someone's Mommy,
I'm not even a wife,

I'm no longer the professional I was all my life,

Well, ye naysayers, harken to the message
I imparted.

Cause this here old "has-been" is just getting started.

IF ONLY....

I've lived long, I've lived fully,

      and I've travelled a lot.

But I haven't hit yet that big jackpot.

Before the rest of my life ends its final unfold,

There is still one sight, I would like to behold.

No, I don't want to see

the Pyramids built by the Egyptian slaves,

I don't want to see

Lenin's and Tutankhamun's graves,

I don't want to see

China's most miraculous "Great Wall,"

I don't want to see

Dubai's "Grand Shopping Mall."

I don't want to see

the Caspian Sea (which is really a Lake,)

I just want to see...100 candles on my

Birthday Cake!

THE CURE

When my happy smile morphs into a frown,

Because the skies turned grey, and I'm feeling down,

When I get that need to express my voice,

My options become a "one-two" choice:

A. I can ask my analyst if he has some time,

or

B. I can take pen in hand and create a rhyme.

At a therapy session I can delve much deeper,

But writing a poem does the job – and it's a helluva lot

cheaper!

IN MEMORIAM

I may have failed in other areas,

but I hope that in the end,

Someone will stand up and say,

"She was a really good friend."

THE READING HOUR

I hope you won't think

that I am being foolish–

Or even worse - that I am being ghoulish.

Cause whether it's Mary's, or Perry's,

or Jerry's, or Kerry's or Sheri's, or Terry's ,

I just love reading their obituaries!

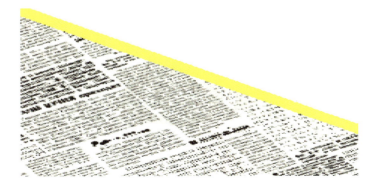

HAPPY AS A CLAM

What clam?

The one that lives in the deep, deep sea?

As I guzzle my bowl of Chowder,

that clam doesn't look happy to me!

# #

It's a metadata tag for social media conversation,

Because Tweeters have decreed us
a Hashtag Nation.

But I'm so out of touch, I'm definitely old-line,

Cause I still define that symbol as simply
"the number sign."

THE NEW DRESS CODE

With all the beautiful women at the Gala,
I won't compete,

Because I'll be wearing tennis shoes
upon my feet.

Five inch heels? For goodness sake!

They cramp my toes in a torturous ache.

They make me walk like a drunken giraffe,

And they strain the muscles in my calf.

You grouse that my Keds are improper to wear.

While that may be true, I'm too old to care.

100 SHADES OF GREY

I was always relaxed, mellow, laid back,

For being happy-go-lucky, I had the knack.

But now I seem to fret all day long,

What if the directions I got are all wrong?

Did I park too far away from the curb?

What if I misread that advertisement blurb?

Did I put enough cash into my wallet?

And did I remember to turn down the

whatchamacallit?

But the biggest worry with which I am smitten,

Is how dreadful is this poem, which I've just written?

SENIOR BALANCE

If I got pulled over and asked to walk

a straight line,

The Officer would give me a huge DUI fine.

Cause I'd teeter and totter and wobble and slink,

Although I hadn't indulged in one single drink!

UP IN THE SKY

"It's a bird, it's a plane..."

then he stopped with a groan,

"Oh s*#t, it's not Superman!!!!

It's only a drone."

THE LINE FORMS HERE

As I paraded through life,
I always wanted to be first.
If that bubble of romance
was about to burst,

I'd break up with Mr. Big,
before he did it to me.
When I saw the curtain coming down,
I was the first to flee,

And when I realized at my job,
I was a dismal misfit,
I'd broach my boss before I got fired,
to announce, "I quit!"

But I have a new mantra,
which I want to broadcast:
When that eternal chariot arrives,
I wanna be last!

A GOOD TIME WAS HAD BY ALL

When the Master Artist, my Final Picture draws,

I know that "died of boredom" will not be its cause.

I will happily proclaim, as I take it in stride,

"The time that I spent here was one helluva ride!"

Made in the USA
Lexington, KY
10 July 2014